People and Friends Remember Me

Veloisa Diana Simpson

Published and Distributed by:
Professional Publishing House
1425 W. Manchester Ave., Suite B
Los Angeles, California 90047
www.professionalpublishinghouse.com
email: professionalpublishinghouse@yahoo.com
(323) 750-3592

First printing:
ISBN: 978-0-9861557-0-3
Library of Congress Control Number:
10987654321

I apply my talents and ability to writing, and I am successful. My writing is more than a source of supply; it is also a source of fulfillment. My writing gives me the opportunity to use the talents and abilities God has given me. Writing gives me a sense of accomplishment. I have put my heart into my writing, knowing that it's from the inside.

SMILE!!

My mind and heart are open to unlimited possibilities. An open door is an invitation to the unknown. Life presents many open doors, so I keep my mind and heart open to possibilities. I find that many doors open to good. I view each open door as an opportunity to grow spiritually, intellectually and emotionally. I know that good awaits me, and I am eager to discover it. I look forward to seeing open doors wherever I go.

SMILE!!

I may feel powerless in certain difficult situations, but powerlessness is an illusion. Even though I may not know how I will find my way through, I know that true wisdom and power come from Spirit within. I fully use the power of Spirit within me to be free from restraint. I break through chains that bind me, and I am open to the understanding that I have the power here. I will be guided as to how to do all things.

Filled with spirit, my life is bursting with God's promises.

SMILE!!

Martin Luther King, Jr. lived a life of service. I commit to be of service. I look for opportunities to help others. I will take right action and lead by example. I speak words that are uplifting and encouraging. I seek ways to build up, rather than to tear down. All acts of service, large or small, help to lift up humankind. I strive for excellence in giving to others from the love of God within me.

SMILE!!

I honor what has been and welcome what is to come. I give thanks for the year that is ending, for all my experiences, and the growth of my soul. I am ready to say good-bye to past events, the challenges that strengthen my faith, and the blissful moments that made me whole. I create a personal ceremony for letting go. I pour out the past. With each gentle breath, I release everything to God. Reverently, I let go. I feel lighter in mind, body, and soul.

On the threshold of a new beginning, I am ready to welcome new growth. I am cleansed, refreshed, and optimistic. I am grateful and open to God's good.

SMILE!!

remember what is true, good, and holy. Every day happenings may trigger old feelings, images or responses. While some of these memories may be sweet and joyful, others may feel painful or challenging. As memories come up, I sense faithfully in Spirit, acknowledge the feelings, and let them go.

I remember who I truly am: My inheritance in wholeness, love, property, and joy. The past no longer has any power over me. I claim my good in full, right here and now.

SMILE!!

The spirit of God is with me through the stormy times of my life. The spirit of God is like the sun that shines even on a rainy day. It is merely hidden behind the clouds in troubled times; my thoughts may turn cloudy with doubt and fear. If I feel separated from God, my hope may begin to fade.

At such times, I turn within. I rest in quiet prayer and meditation. I gently release any sense of separation. I affirm that God is my ever-present source of hope. I hear the still, small voice within. It whispers, "God's in the rain." This truth washes over me and cleanses me of fear. The renewing light of God shines through me like the rays of the sun. Spiritual light radiates from within, and my hope is restored.

SMILE!!

I honor what has been and welcome what is to come. I am ready to say good-bye to the past events, the challenges that strengthened my faith and the blissful moments that made me whole.

I create a personal ceremony for letting go. I imagine myself as a sacred vessel from which I pour out the past. With each gentle breath, I release everything to God. Reverently, I let go. I feel lighter in mind, body and soul. I rest in the holy emptiness, trusting spirit to fill it with love.

SMILE!!

*Y*esterday is gone and tomorrow has not yet begun. Today is here. How will I make this day count? What thoughts will I hold in mind? What tasks will I accomplish? How many lives will I touch?

Life is lived day by day, moment by moment. When I look at my life, I see a tapestry. Each experience is interwoven in a pattern that is uniquely mine. The overall design emerges more every day. I do not need to worry about tomorrow! Instead, I joyously live for today and look forward to the blessings that unfold, revealing the beautiful tapestry of my life.

Today, I hold the intention to create wonderful moments. I chance to bless others and experience the greatness of God.

SMILE!!

*W*hat must I do to earn the love of God? NOTHING! God's love is already mine. No one and nothing can limit or restrict it. I need only open my heart and mind to receive unconditional love and allow myself to experience God's grace.

Grace is demonstrated in the beauty of nature, in unexpected good, in feeling my oneness with spirit. In God's grace, I am divinely guided, protected, and comforted. Grace softens my struggles and takes me beyond my self-imposed limitations, filling my mind with divine ideas and my life with serenity. As I appreciated the activity of God in my life, I learn to trust in its continuing expression, and I soar in God's grace.

SMILE!!

*G*iving and receiving go hand in hand. I give to others, and I'm also receptive to the good that is shared with me. I allow others the joy of giving by graciously welcoming and accepting compliments, material gifts, and suggestions. I accept blessings in whatever form they may appear. I open my mind and heart to joy, love, prosperity, and all the good in life. I may have overlooked certain blessings before because they showed up in unexpected ways.

I gratefully and graciously embrace every blessing in my life.

SMILE!!

*L*ife is full of joy and sorrow, but no condition is beyond the comfort of spirit. Whatever my experience, even before I voice my prayer, the comfort I seek is available to me. I have what I need for any situation. I ask and receive.

No request is too great or too small. Each one invites answers, abundance, and comforts to arise within me. All that I need is available for me to claim in this very moment. Spirit in me is my comfort, inspiration, and guidance to manifest what I need. Gratitude fills my heart as I know my needs are met.

God is my comfort and refuge!

SMILE!!

I spread joy by sharing a positive attitude, a smile, openness, and appreciation, for all of life's blessings. I am blessed in so many ways, and I rejoice with the glow of spirit. If others are pessimistic or glum, I do not take on their mood, but rather hold a positive thought for them, knowing this too shall pass. Instead of finding fault or complaint, I look for the best in each person.

Goodness abounds as I open my eyes to witness it. The blessings of God, I now see in my life, fill my mind and heart with joy and thanksgiving. I give of my happiness freely, spreading the good I see and have. With energy and exhilaration, I inspire those around me. Joy is contagious.

SMILE!!

*I*f an unsettling experience occurs, I turn inward in search for answers. Calmly and confidently, I become still and focus on my breathing and heartbeat. With each steady breath and orderly heartbeat, I become aware of divine order in me. As I identify this natural expression of order in my body, I recognize that divine order underlies all of life as a solid foundation. I experience peace. I ask for and receive wisdom and understanding. I see the events of my life are unfolding in perfect order. My path and purpose are clear. Divine order manifests in my life with ease and grace.

SMILE!!

*P*ain may be part of life, but suffering is optional. We suffer when we feel unloved, unprotected or perceive life as hostile. If I ever turn to the truth, there is only one Power God, the Good. During hard times, I seek the spirit of God in me.

I build an internal fortress of truth that withstands any fear, anxiety, or distress. In the silence, I take refuge from any struggle or suffering. I abide in comfort, joy and peace beyond any circumstances. One with God, I am always protected.

SMILE!!

There are plenty of smiles for all of us …

KEEP SMILING!!!

SMILE!!

I praise others and am blessed in return. Children shine when they are praised by parents, teachers, and loved ones. They beam with pride when they are told they have done well, or when they are recognized for their talents. Although I am now an adult, I react in the same way when I am praised. I feel a sense of pride when others acknowledge my skills. I can give that satisfaction to others by praising them so they, too, feel appreciated. I make a conscious effort to praise others. I point out their strengths and recognize their abilities. We all enjoy being acknowledged for our uniqueness. I appreciate others, remembering what a joy it is to be praised.

SMILE!!

*L*ife is the power of God at work, constantly flowing in the present moment. With my mind and heart, I have the power to connect with spirit and co-create a blissful life. I start by expressing gratitude for existence. I ask for the right guidance, and write down the dreams of my heart. I follow God's direction in each step and express gratitude for my life as it unfolds.

SMILE!!

There is nothing like a good laugh to make me feel refreshed, free and joyful. In the presence of laughter, worries or stress melt away. When I laugh with others, I feel connected to them. I take everything less seriously. I open, soften, and embrace the joy that is everywhere present. I look around and see the humor in life.

Laughter arises and I open myself to express it. My burdens lighten and my spirit is lifted. My laugh comes as easily as the joyful giggle of a care-free child. I am happily sharing my good energy with others. My heart is cheerful and I live in joy.

SMILE!!

I treasure all of my learning experiences. Learning is a treasure that will follow me everywhere. All my triumphs and tribulations are to be treasured. With each experience, I learn more about myself and my purpose. With every situation, I see the world from a new perspective, and I grow.

Each stage of my life has its challenges and rewards. It brings wisdom and insight. How exciting to know life's lessons are unfolding. How wonderful that each day inspires new growth! My life is not stagnant or dull, but filled with new joys. I look forward to each day, ready to learn about myself and the world. I treasure my life and all its lessons.

SMILE!!

To matter the date on my birth certificate, I am ageless! My life is renewed with every breath, with every new moment. I do not allow my biological age to define or restrict me. In spirit, I am unlimited and fully capable of great achievements, no matter when I was born.

I gently relinquish my fears I may have about the aging process. I do not lament natural changes taking place in my body. I remain young at heart by maintaining a positive attitude, which inspires me to think, act, and appear youthful. I am free to live a joyful, graceful, and continually refreshed life, for at any age…

I am ageless….

SMILE!!

Take care of your thoughts;

.... they become your words.

Take care of your words;

.... they become your actions.

Take care of your actions;

.... they become your habits.

Take care of your habits;

.... they become your character.

Take care of your character;

.... it becomes your destiny.

SMILE!!

*F*reedom is a state of being beyond external circumstances. I can experience freedom, regardless of what I see outside myself. I choose to be positive in my thoughts, feelings, attitudes and perceptions. By choosing to focus on the good, I am free. I release negative thoughts and emotions; and feel lighter in mind, body, and soul. I nurture my mind with ideas of health and well-being. I experience the freedom of a balanced and productive life. My outlook is positive. I expect only good.

Freedom is a choice, a state of mind. By holding positive thoughts and feelings, I experience life to the fullest. I choose to be optimistic.

I choose my freedom...

SMILE!!

I am holding on for time

Holding for wisdom

Holding on for strength

Holding on for energy

SMILE!!

When I reach out to life, life always reaches out to me. I appreciate my progress, as I contemplate where I have been and what I have accomplished. I awaken to and appreciate the progress I have made. I may not have reached my full potential yet, but I can appreciate every phase of my journey's past, present, and future. Each step forward deepens the meaning and purpose of life. I need not rush or force my progress. I am one with the one presence in everything that is and will be.

Knowing I am divinely supported, I relax and enjoy life's abundant opportunities to learn and grow.

SMILE!!

J am grateful for acts of generosity that have supported me in times of need. I have known the gift of an encouraging word or an unexpected opportunity. So I reciprocate and give to others. The more freely I give to life, the more freely life gives back to me.

SMILE!!

I am a beautiful child of God, living in a beautiful world. My body is a holy temple. My mind is a powerful tool. My heart is an open vessel. I give thanks for the beauty of the world around me, from the smallest atom to the grandest mountain range.

I know that beauty is divinely created, just as I am. I am a creative, confident person, blessed with the spirit to accomplish all that I believe is possible. I am the unique, beautiful person I am meant to be.

SMILE!!

Self-care is a way of life. Overall, well-being is supported by good habits that nurture my spiritual, physical, mental, and emotional health. Caring for me means making healthy and harmonious choices. When I take care of myself, I eat nutritious foods in appropriate amounts, enjoy restorative sleep, and keep my body and my mind active and nimble.

My body is a blessing from God. I listen to its needs and love it unconditionally. I feed my soul through meditation.

SMILE!!

The joy of spirit is with me always. My joy comes from trusting God. As God's child, my true nature is to be joyous. I am cheerful and happy. I radiate joy to everyone I meet. Joy sustains my soul, strengthens and heals my body, and harmonized my relationships. I am blessed by the joy of spirit.

SMILE!!

Friendship is a mirror. Throughout my life, I have countless opportunities to be a friend and to make new friends. Each friendship is an occasion to experience God in action. I want to behold kindness, peace, happiness, and love in each person I meet. Each friendship is also an opportunity for me to reveal my highest and best qualities. My friends know and love me. My spirits are lifted by their presence.

I gladly reciprocate. Each friend is a blessing in my life. I thank God for my friends.

SMILE!!

J give generously from my heart. Christmas time is a joyous season of goodwill. Generosity is a time when the giving spirit is flowing freely. I am generous in thoughts, words, actions, and attitudes. In helping a neighbor, sharing gifts with friends, contributing to charitable organizations, I share from the heart. I generously give by being kind and loving, and by praying for anyone in need when he comes to my mind and heart. The ways in which I can be generous are endless. I make it my loving task to express generosity. As I do, I know that I am a blessing to myself and to others.

SMILE!!

*I*n the silence of prayer, I acknowledge that I am in the flow of divine order that is moving in and through all life. I am committed to being there for a child who needs guidance, love, and assurance. I am ready to be of service to a neighbor who is praying for a helping hand. I am open to spending time with someone who simply needs interaction with a caring person. I am where I need to be to give and to receive a blessing.

SMILE!!

The wisdom of God is within me to make wise and right judgments. I embrace supportive friends and people, inspiring places and productive ideas. My mind, heart, and life are guided by the wisdom of God.

SMILE!!

Giving generously and abundantly, my heart is a bushel basket, which overflows with love and generosity to my friends and organizations. I am grateful for the abundant blessings in my life.

SMILE!!

*I*f I take a step backward, I hope to take three steps forward. Happy is dealing with the moments and enjoying them.

SMILE!!

I am kind and loving to myself and others. Kindness is a choice. It cost nothing, yet it is wonderfully fulfilling. When I treat others with kindness, I feel better about myself. Every act of kindness, large or small, produces joy, peace, and happiness. Any person I meet may carry a burden inside. A simple, heartfelt smile may bring them hope. Opening a door, saying "hello," and offering a helping hand may make a major difference in someone's day. I also remember to be kind to myself. If I criticize my looks, actions, or thoughts, I stop and find one aspect of myself that I like.

As I choose kindness, I am rewarded with love, peace, patience, and joy.

Love is .... PATIENT

Love is .... NOT BOASTFUL

Love is .... KIND

Love is ....NOT RUDE

Love is ....NOT ENVIOUS

SMILE!!

One of the most viable messages Jesus shared was a simple invitation to be a peacemaker. Every person is created of God with the potential to be a peacemaker. We have spiritual power, and through our peaceful thoughts, words, and actions, we can create a peaceful world.

Whatever may be occurring near to me or across the globe, I maintain an awareness of peace. The peace of God can be known and recognized in all situations. It is brought into an expression as serenity, trust, goodwill, and friendship. Through prayer, I think peace, speak peace, and act in ways that foster peace.

I am a peacemaker!

SMILE!!

*W*hen I put God first in my life, I know only peace. When the unconditional love of God fills my thoughts, it leaves no space for separation or judgment. When I see others through the eyes of peace and love, I contribute to world peace.

I begin my day by thanking God for the peace in me. Before I go to sleep, I acknowledge that peace also lies within everyone on Earth.

SMILE!!

My Affirmations

Inner Peace ~

The light-filled presence of God stirs within my soul. I am at peace.

Guidance ~

Divine light within and around me leads me on the path of good.

Healing ~

I am one with God's healing energy. I am filled with strength and vitality.

Prosperity ~

> *Divine abundance overflows into every area of my life. Prosperity is mine.*

World Peace ~

> *I greet each day with <u>Faith</u> and <u>Hope,</u> as I hold a vision of peace for the world.*

SMILE!!

We all want to be appreciated and loved by others; but a need for approval can be a stumbling block. I pray to fully love myself as I am. I pray to accept the love of God. I pray to appreciate my gifts and the unique desires of my heart that God gave me. As I learn to love myself, my need for admiration and outside approval diminishes. I am whole and complete, just as I am.

SMILE!!

I honor my ageless nature by living with enthusiasm and gratitude. The essence of my being is ageless. The spark of divinity of God within me is everlasting. It was there before my birth and will continue beyond my physical body. What a blessing it is to know that this most real part of me is always fresh and vibrant.

As I cherish memories, I gain wisdom, growth, and a bounty of lessons learned throughout my life. I understand that my fundamental nature remains ageless. No matter what my chronological age is, my spirit is anew and a budding leaf. I visualize myself in a flow of all that God is. I honor my ageless nature by living this day with enthusiasm and gratitude.

SMILE!!

45

*M*y prosperity is not only about the level of my financial success or the quantity or quality of material possessions. My experience of prosperity moves beyond the physical to the divine. God's blessings are endless, abundantly evident and available to me at all times and in all circumstances.

God is my source and my substance. I am divinely supported with all that I need to live a full and prosperous life. Clarity and direction, compassion and forgiveness, peace and serenity, creativity and energy; as well as my physical needs and materials comforts are mine in abundance. Each of these gifts and so many more are here for me now. Divine abundance overflows into every area of my life. *PROSPERITY IS MINE.*

SMILE!!

I live my truth by knowing who I am and the values I hold dear. My values are reflected in all I think, say, and do. If I am ever afraid to follow my heart or speak my truth, I remember strength and courage come from within. My life is a reflection of my truth, and I live it with passion and conviction.

SMILE!!

All my life I've been trying to find the TRUTH to make it BEAUTIFUL.

SMILE!!

Pay attention to what's going on.

SMILE!!

$\mathcal{A}$s a new year begins, I focus on my life, where I have been, and where I see myself going.

I review my accomplishments and mistakes with honesty:

- What am I most proud of?
- What do I want to change and how?

I begin by accepting my current circumstances honestly. Each year brings unlimited possibilities to write a new story.

I am true to myself and I focus on what is really important. From this awareness, I create an authentic life that reflects who I truly am. I am unique. My life is unique. I am the creator, director, and writer of my story. I direct it in a way that brings the greatest joy for me and others. As I live authentically, I enjoy a life of well-being and love.

SMILE!!

Remember the SMILING

Remember the LAUGHING

Remember the TALKING

Remember the SHARING

Remember the CARING
and LOVING

Remember the GOOD TIMES always

SMILE!!

www.ingramcontent.com/pod-product-compliance
Lightning Source LLC
Chambersburg PA
CBHW070830100426
42813CB00003B/556